UNSOLVED

# BERMUDA TRIANGLE

DINAH WILLIAMS

Children's Press®

An imprint of Scholastic Inc.

A special thank-you to our team of fact-checkers.



Library of Congress Cataloging-in-Publication Data available

ISBN 978-1-5461-7853-8 (library binding) | ISBN 978-1-5461-7854-5 (paperback)

10 9 8 7 6 5 4 3 2 1 26 27 28 29 30

Printed in China 62

First edition, 2026

Book design by Kay Petronio

Photos ©: back cover background: Chris Clor/Getty Images; back cover top: VICTOR HABBICK VISIONS/Science Photo Library/Getty Images; 2–3: Chris Clor/Getty Images; 4: VICTOR HABBICK VISIONS/Science Source; 5: Jim McMahon/Mapman ®; 8: mikroman6/Getty Images; 9: Alessandro Lonati. All rights reserved 2025/Bridgeman Images; 12: Peter Dennis/Getty Images; 13: Look and Learn/Bridgeman Images; 14–15: Look and Learn/Illustrated Papers Collection/Bridgeman Images; 17: Cavan Images/Getty Images; 18–19, 20–21: U.S. Naval History and Heritage Command/Navy.mil; 24–25: Acey Harper/Getty Images; 26: Courtesy of the NAS Fort Lauderdale Museum; 27: National Archives and Records Administration; 28: VICTOR HABBICK VISIONS/Science Photo Library/Getty Images; 29 all: Courtesy of the NAS Fort Lauderdale Museum; 30: Smith Archive/Alamy Images; 31: Chronicle/Alamy Images; 33: Mark Stevenson/Getty Images; 34: Sandi Smolker/Getty Images; 35: Science Channel/YouTube; 36: John Lund/Getty Images; 37: guvendemir/Getty Images; 38: Marcoriveroph/Getty Images; 43: EyeEm Mobile GmbH/Getty Images; 44 top left: Alessandro Lonati. All rights reserved 2025/Bridgeman Images; 44 top center: U.S. Naval History and Heritage Command/Navy.mil; 44 top right: Courtesy of the NAS Fort Lauderdale Museum; 44 bottom left: Peter Dennis/Getty Images; 44 bottom right: U.S. Naval History and Heritage Command/Navy.mil; 45 bottom left: Smith Archive/Alamy Images; 45 bottom right: Susan & Allan Parker/Alamy Images; 46 top: NASA/JPL/NIMA; 46 bottom: Buena Vista Images/Getty Images.

All other photos © Shutterstock.

INTRODUCTION

# BEWARE OF BERMUDA

There is a mysterious place in the Atlantic Ocean. It is known as the Bermuda Triangle. Strange and powerful storms seem to appear out of nowhere. Travelers can quickly find themselves in trouble. Sailors and pilots have reported that their equipment stops working.

More than fifty ships and twenty airplanes have disappeared there. What happened to them? Investigators can't explain where some of them went. There are **theories**, but no one knows for sure.

The triangle lies between Florida and the islands of Bermuda and Puerto Rico.

This stretch of the ocean can be dangerous. There have been reports of huge waves. The waves can reach heights of up to 100 feet (30 m). The wind can change direction without warning. Some claim to have seen strange fog. Others have seen fire! Is it just the weather, or is it something **supernatural**?

Some people believe this area is cursed. Others think that aliens may have taken those who disappeared. Let's explore what we know about this mystery!

Vincent Gaddis wrote an article in *Argosy* magazine in 1964. It was about ships that disappeared in the Atlantic. He named the area the "Bermuda Triangle."

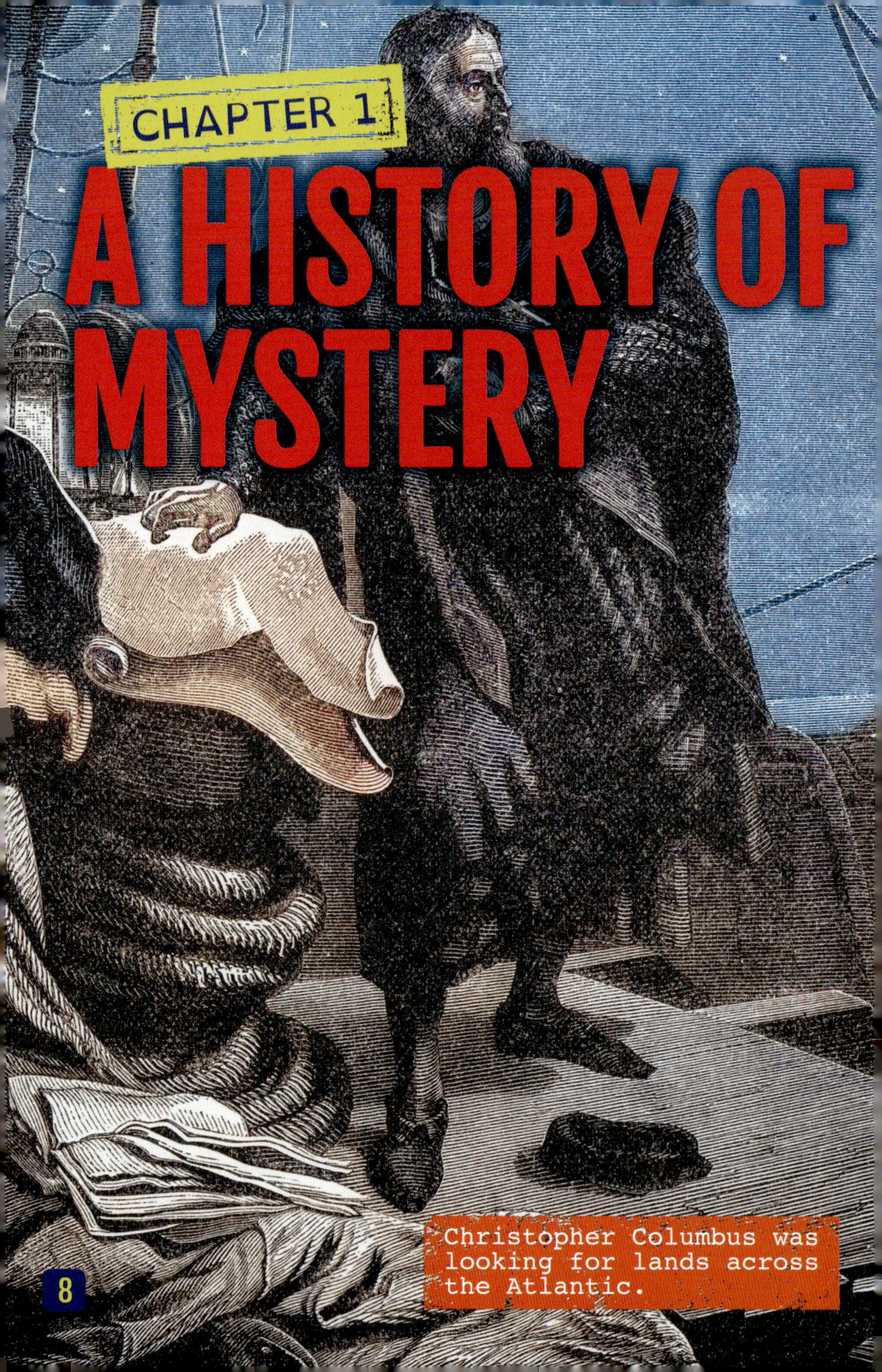

CHAPTER 1

# A HISTORY OF MYSTERY

Christopher Columbus was looking for lands across the Atlantic.

Christopher Columbus was an explorer. He was one of the first people to write about the Bermuda Triangle. In 1492, Columbus's three ships traveled through the area. They were the *Niña*, the *Pinta*, and the *Santa María*.

Suddenly, the wind stopped. The ships slowed to a halt. Their **compasses** stopped working. The ships sat there for days. The crew became nervous in the strange seas.

These are Columbus's three ships. The *Santa María* was the largest.

The crew also noticed thick brown clumps in the water. It was floating seaweed. They called it sargassum, after a plant from their country. They feared it would tangle up the boats and drag them underwater.

Columbus wrote about other strange sights. He saw creepy lights and a burst of flames. The crew was relieved when the wind picked up. They sailed on.

This is floating sargassum.

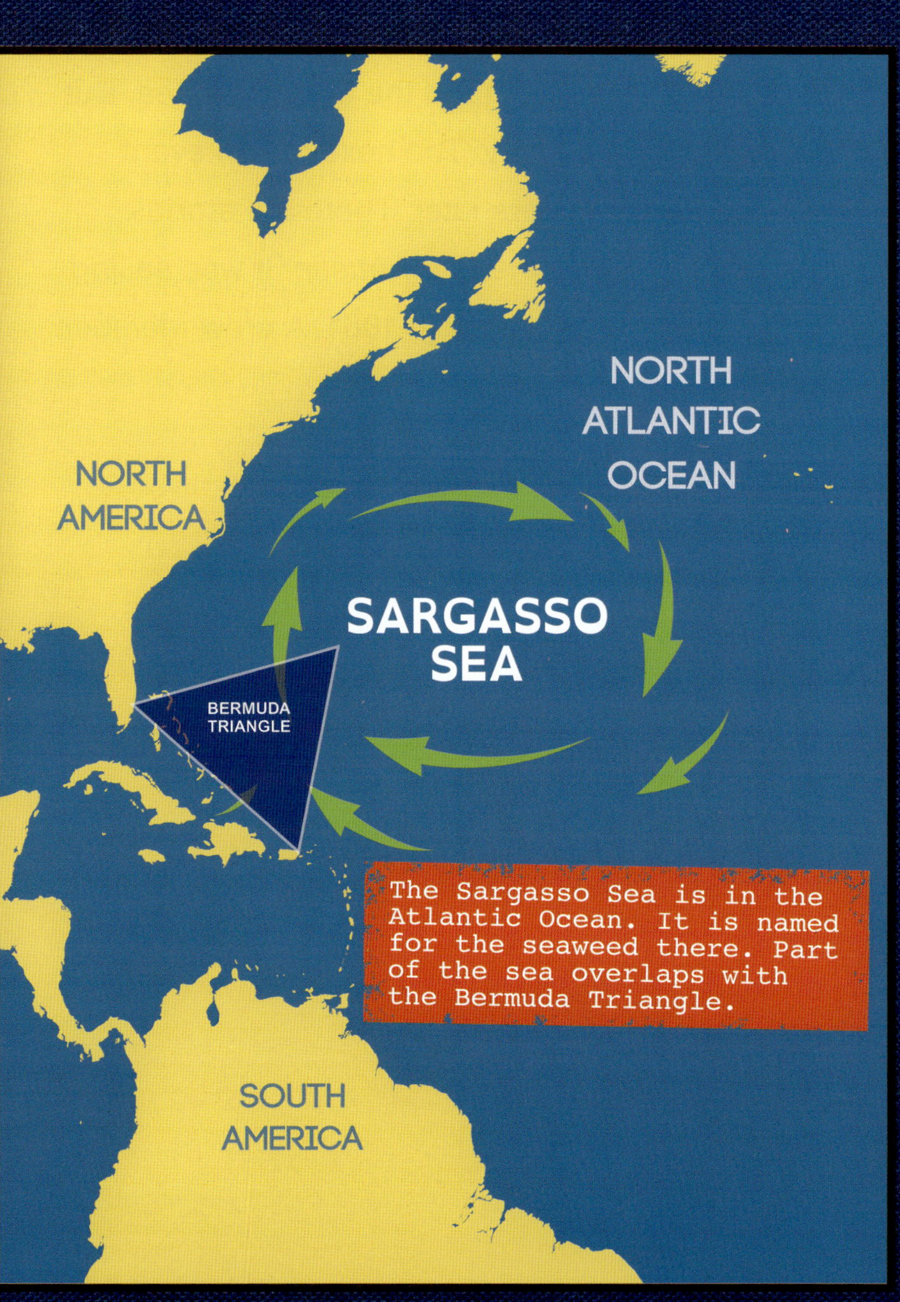


The Sargasso Sea is in the Atlantic Ocean. It is named for the seaweed there. Part of the sea overlaps with the Bermuda Triangle.

Columbus's ships escaped the Sargasso Sea. But others weren't so lucky. The next known event was hundreds of years later. There are stories about a ship called the *Ellen Austin*. It was sailing from London to New York in 1881. A crew member spotted another ship on the water.

The *Ellen Austin* was 210 feet (64 m) long. That is about the same length as a child taking 120 steps!

The captain shown here is holding a spyglass.

The captain of the *Ellen Austin* looked through his spyglass. No one seemed to be on board the other vessel. But he waited two days before getting closer. He feared it could be a pirate ship.

The captain sent a few of his crew over to the ship in a rowboat. The ship was empty! There was no crew. It didn't make sense. The ship was in good condition. It had food and supplies stored.

The men chosen to take over a captured ship were called a prize crew.

But the name of the ship had been scraped off. And the captain's log was missing. A log is a ship's record of its speed and progress. Why was the ship abandoned?

A "ghost ship" is the name for one found drifting without a crew.

The captain could get money for the ship. Some of his crew stayed on board. The two ships began sailing to New York.

They soon ran into some bad weather. The ships were separated. The captain spotted the second ship a few days later. It was empty! His crew had vanished. They were never found.

# SHIPWRECK RECORD

There have been more than 300 recorded shipwrecks around the island of Bermuda. That is more than any other place in the world per square mile. This island is surrounded by **coral reefs**. It is believed the reefs are one of the causes.

This is a photo of a shipwreck. It is off the coast of Bermuda. The dark spots in the water are parts of a coral reef.

# CHAPTER 2
# MORE LEGENDS OF LOST SHIPS

In 1918, there was another strange disappearance. It happened during World War I. The USS *Cyclops* was a huge ship with more than 300 sailors on board. It left Barbados in March. Barbados is a small island southeast of Puerto Rico.

You can see some of the sailors on the USS *Cyclops* here. "USS" means a United States Ship in the Navy.

The ship was heading to the United States. Then it crossed into the Bermuda Triangle. The last message from the ship was "Weather Fair, All Well." No one on the ship radioed for help. The ship was never seen again.

The US Navy searched for the lost ship. But there was no evidence that the *Cyclops* sank. Nothing was left behind. The wreck has never been found. Was it taken by an enemy during the war? To this day, no one knows.

The USS *Nereus* sank shortly after America entered World War II.

Two sister ships of the *Cyclops* met the same fate. The USS *Proteus* vanished in the Bermuda Triangle in November 1941. One month later, the USS *Nereus* disappeared. Both ships and their crews were never seen again.

Another mysterious disappearance happened on December 22, 1967. Daniel Burack invited Reverend Patrick Horgan to go out on his boat. It was named *Witchcraft*. They planned to look at the Christmas lights on the Florida coast.

Burack sent out a distress call at 9:00 p.m. The US Coast Guard arrived at the boat's location in less than twenty minutes. But the boat was nowhere to be found. Investigators were puzzled. The expensive cruiser was supposed to be unsinkable. And a massive search turned up nothing.

This boat looks similar to the *Witchcraft*.

Daniel Burack (left) and Reverend Patrick Horgan

The *Witchcraft* had built-in flotation. The main part of the boat was designed not to sink.

# CHAPTER 3
# THE SKIES ABOVE

Ships aren't the only vehicles that have been lost in the Bermuda Triangle. Planes have also disappeared there. There was a group of five United States Navy aircraft based in Fort Lauderdale, Florida. The aircraft and 14 pilots were known as Flight 19.

This was a Naval Air Station in Florida. Flight 19 took off from there.

On December 5, 1945, the pilots took off for a two-hour training mission. Flight 19 was headed toward Bermuda. The group was led by Lieutenant Charles Taylor, an experienced pilot. The weather was fine except for a little rain.

The pilots flew out to sea and dropped their practice bombs. Then something strange happened. One of the pilots was heard saying, "I don't know where we are. We must have gotten lost after that last turn."

A nearby Navy pilot heard Flight 19's radio messages. Taylor said, "Both my compasses are out, and I am trying to find Fort Lauderdale, Florida." But Flight 19 was flying in the opposite direction. The planes were headed farther out to sea. They were running low on fuel. Taylor told his men they may need to crash-land in the ocean.

Lieutenant Charles Taylor

These are Navy Avenger planes. They are the same kind that disappeared in 1945.

The Navy launched two rescue planes. They flew to the last known position of Flight 19. But all five planes were gone. Then one of the rescue planes also disappeared. Crew members on a passing ship reported seeing flames and an oil slick in the water. The Coast Guard and the Navy searched for five days. They didn't find any trace of Flight 19 or the rescue plane.

Some believe the rescue plane may have blown up. "They just vanished," one of the rescuers later said. "And nobody ever found the bodies or any **debris**."

Burt E. Baluk

Joseph Tipton Bossi

George F. Devlin

Sergeant Robert F. Gallivan

2nd Lieutenant Forrest J. Gerber

Private Robert F. Gruebel

William E. Lightfoot

Sergeant George R. Paonessa

Walter R. Palpart, Jr.

Captain Edward J. Powers

Captain George W. Stivers

Herman A. Thelander

Sergeant Howell O. Thompson

Taylor and these 13 pilots from Flight 19 were never heard from again.

This is one of the last images of the *Star Tiger*. It was traveling from London to Bermuda.

Another flight disappeared in 1948. The *Star Tiger* was on its way to Bermuda. The plane vanished along with its thirty-one passengers. They were never heard from again.

One year later, the *Star Ariel* met the same fate. It took off from Bermuda. Soon after, the plane and its twenty passengers vanished. The cause of both disappearances is still unknown.

How could so many ships and planes vanish in the area? Was there something supernatural about this stretch of sea? Some people thought so.

This is what the *Star Ariel* looked like.

CHAPTER 4

# FACT OR FICTION?

Atlantis is a fictional underwater island. It is a Greek myth.

In 1974, Charles Berlitz wrote a book. He had a theory. He believed the lost city of Atlantis was under the Bermuda Triangle. Berlitz said that energy from the city caused the disappearances. There is no evidence that Atlantis existed. But some people believed him.

Since then, there have been other theories. Some people think that aliens use the Bermuda Triangle to access our planet. They collect our planes and ships for research. Do you think that's possible?

Many UFO sightings have been reported over the Bermuda Triangle. But this image is not real.

Years went by with more reports of missing ships and planes. But there were explanations for all. Until a small plane carrying three people disappeared in June 2005. It was lost between the Bahamas and Florida. The Bahamas is an island country within the Bermuda Triangle. The plane and the passengers were never found.

The missing plane from 2005 was a Piper, like this one.

A diver examines a shipwreck off the coast of Florida.

This was probably the last reported unsolved disappearance. Why? Because the equipment on ships and planes has improved. Sea and air travel are safer. Search and rescue missions are also more successful now.

Giant waves like these can easily sink a ship.

Facts can explain some of the disappearances in the Bermuda Triangle. The area is one of the busiest shipping routes in the world. More ships mean more shipwrecks.

Dangerous weather often occurs in the Bermuda Triangle. This includes hurricanes and sea tornadoes. Storms like these can cause planes to crash. They can also create giant waves that are big enough to sink a ship.

The **Gulf Stream** runs through the Bermuda Triangle. It can cause storms. It can also cause strong ocean **currents**. Currents can carry a wreck far from where searchers are looking.

The deepest part of the Atlantic Ocean is located in the Bermuda Triangle. The Puerto Rico Trench is 28,374 feet (8,648 m) below the surface. That is almost the height of Mount Everest. Finding anything at that depth is nearly impossible.

There are an estimated 300 shipwrecks in the Bermuda Triangle.

# THE WRONG DIRECTION

The Bermuda Triangle contains a special **magnetic field**. A compass shows which direction is north. The Triangle's magnetic field can cause a compass's needle to move in the wrong direction. No wonder people kept getting lost!

The needle on a compass is a small magnet.

A methane explosion can be dangerous for passing ships.

Another possible reason for ships sinking in the area is **methane**. Methane is normally a gas. But it becomes solid when it is deep in the cold ocean. Some scientists believe that pieces of methane can break off from the seafloor.

The solid methane becomes gas again as it rises. The gas could burst out of the ocean. Methane can also catch fire. This fiery explosion could sink a ship.

This illustration shows an underwater gas fire.

# WHAT TO BELIEVE?

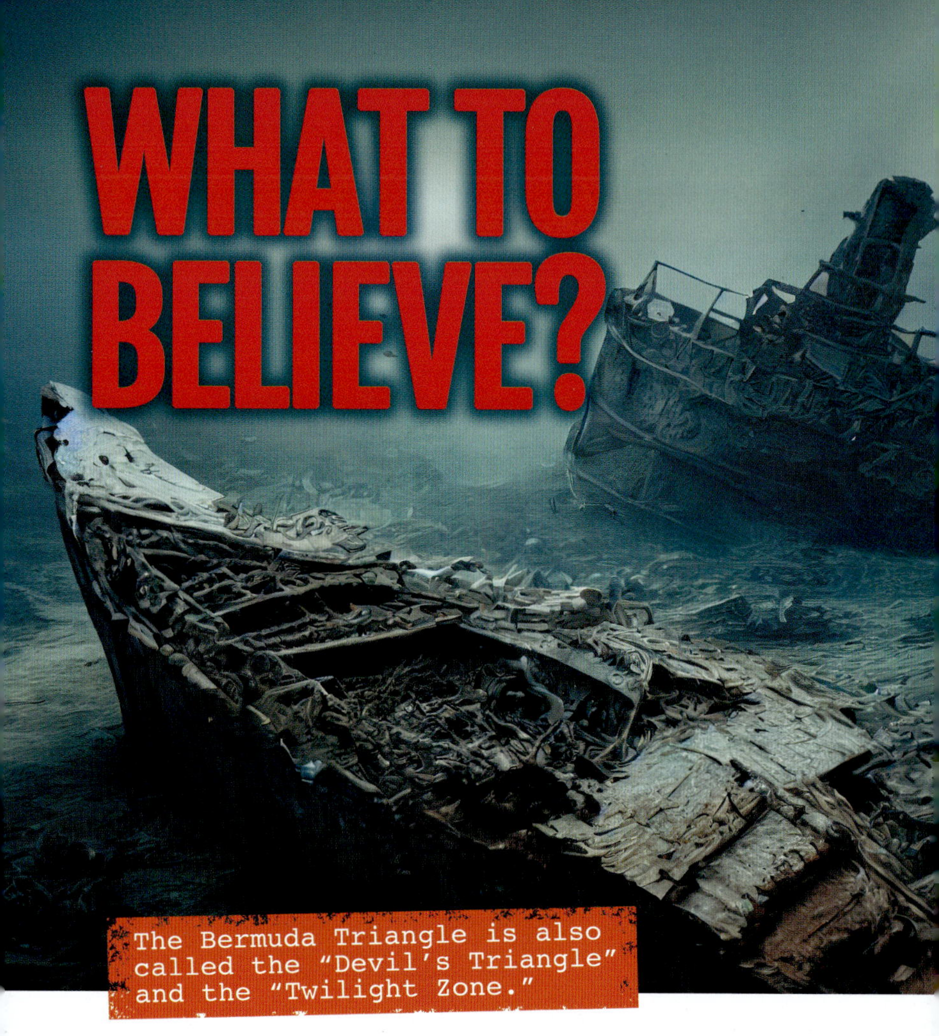

The Bermuda Triangle is also called the "Devil's Triangle" and the "Twilight Zone."

More than seventy ships and planes have been lost in the Bermuda Triangle. There are possible explanations for some. But others disappeared under mysterious circumstances. How can a ship or a plane vanish? Will the wreckages ever be found?

Without enough evidence, this mystery may remain unsolved. What do you believe? Maybe you're not sure. What's been lost might never be found. Maybe we'll never know what happened!

Wreck diving is a type of scuba diving. Divers explore the wreckage of ships and planes.

# TIMELINE: Then and Now

**Christopher Columbus's ships get trapped in the Bermuda Triangle.**

**USS *Cyclops* disappears.**

**Five planes of Flight 19 vanish.**

**1492** | **1881** | **1918** | **1941** | **1945**

**Some of the *Ellen Austin* crew is lost on a mysterious ship.**

**USS *Proteus* and USS *Nereus* disappear.**

Vincent Gaddis names the "Bermuda Triangle."

Charles Berlitz's book suggests Atlantis caused the disappearances.

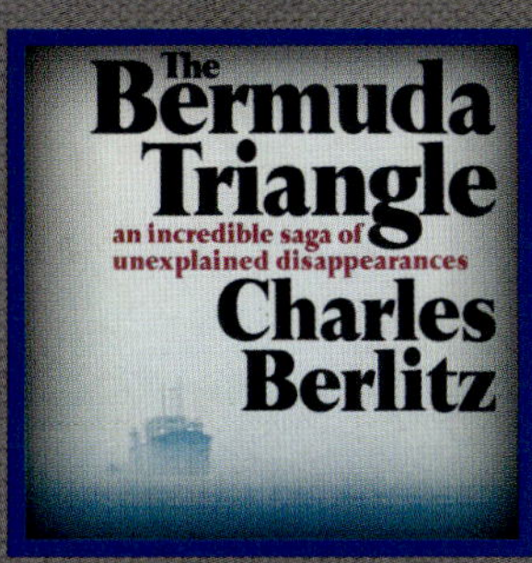


1948 | 1964 | 1967 | 1974 | 2005

The *Star Tiger* is lost on its way to Bermuda.

The *Witchcraft* disappears off the coast of Florida.

A small plane carrying three people vanishes.

# MORE SPOOKY SPOTS

The Bermuda Triangle is not the only mysterious area in the world!

Underwater volcano in the Devil's Sea

Many planes and ships have been lost in the Devil's Sea. It is an area off the southeast coast of Japan. Scientists learned there is a volcano deep under the water. Eruptions could have caused some of the wrecks there.

The coast of Namibia in Africa has dangerous fog. It is hard to see the rocks along the shore. It is called the Skeleton Coast because so many ships have sunk there.

Skeleton Coast

# GLOSSARY

**compass** (KUHM-puhs) an instrument with a magnetic pointer that indicates north, used for finding directions

**coral reef** (KOR-uhl reef) a structure made of coral and other materials that have solidified into rock

**current** (KUR-uhnt) the movement of water in a specific direction in a river or an ocean

**debris** (duh-BREE) the pieces of something that has been broken or destroyed

**Gulf Stream** (guhlf streem) a warm water current that flows across the Atlantic Ocean from the Gulf of Mexico toward Europe

**magnetic field** (mag-NET-ik feeld) the area around a magnet or electric current that has the power to attract other metals, usually iron or steel

**methane** (METH-ane) a colorless, odorless gas that burns easily and is commonly used for fuel

**supernatural** (soo-pur-NACH-ur-uhl) existing outside normal human experience or knowledge

**theory** (THEER-ee) an idea or statement that explains how or why something happens

# INDEX



## ABOUT THE AUTHOR

Dinah Williams, who loves all things spooky and mysterious, has written more than a dozen books for kids, including *Amazing Immortals*; *Terrible but True: Awful Events in American History*; *True Hauntings: Deadly Disasters*; *Spooky Cemeteries*, which won the 2009 Children's Choice Book of the Year Award; and the Unsolved series: *Amelia Earhart*, *Bigfoot*, *Captain Kidd's Treasure*, and *Pyramids of Egypt*.